DIS-
ORGANIZED
CRIME

True Stories of Unlucky Thieves & Stupid Robbers

Compiled and illustrated by
RON BELL

LONGSTREET PRESS
Atlanta, Georgia

Published by
LONGSTREET PRESS, INC.
A subsidiary of Cox Newspapers,
A division of Cox Enterprises, Inc.
2140 Newmarket Parkway
Suite 118
Marietta, GA 30067

Printed in the United States of America

1st printing 1994

Library of Congress Catalog Card Number: 93-81147

ISBN 1-56352-126-1

This book was printed by R. R. Donnelley & Sons, Harrisonburg,
Virginia.

Cover design and illustration by Ron Bell
Book design by Laura McDonald

This book is dedicated to
the memories of Harvey Kurtzman and
William Gaines, whose gifts for seeing the
MADness in everyday life have been an
inspiration to generations.

Introduction

The stories in this book are true. I have not included names so as to protect everyone involved. In some cases where the innocent victims have due reason to be embarrassed, I have even excluded the city name. All of the stories were taken from major news sources by way of newspapers and radio. The fact that the stories are contained in this book does not mean that all the alleged criminals were indicted of their crimes. It only means that at the time of arrest, they were suspected of criminal activity—and they weren't very bright in how they pulled it off. But let's not get too analytical. Just have fun and enjoy the book.

A few stories come from other folks who heard about *Disorganized Crime.* Thanks to George Cochran, Kelley Krahulek, Alan Dittrich, Vicci Wengrzyn, and Merilyn Strong for submitting them to me for the book.

Thanks also to Sharon, Herman, Mark, Robin, and the folks at Longstreet for their help throughout this project.

Miscellaneous Mistakes & Misfits

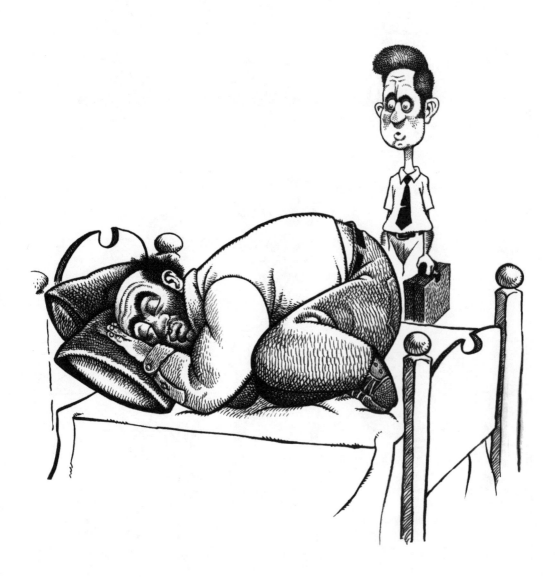

This Bed Is Juuuust Right

As if he had just entered a bad fairy tale, a Dallas, Texas, man came home for lunch to find that someone had broken into his home and eaten all of his food. Hearing a snoring sound coming from his bedroom, the man went to investigate and was astonished to discover a stranger asleep in his bed. Police were called and the man was gently awakened and escorted to jail. Too bad there weren't three bears somewhere in this story.

A Convenient Arrest

A Greenville, South Carolina, convenience store was the scene of a comedy of errors that went on for most of the evening. An armed man entered the store, walked behind the counter, and knocked the cashier to the floor. Two women then came in and the thief tried to pose as the clerk, but couldn't figure out how to open the cash register when ringing up their items. Frustrated, the robber apologized and told them it was all on the house. After the women left, however, he feared they might grow suspicious and turn him in, so he left the store and chased them down the road in his car. He crashed at an intersection not far from the store. At this point (Are you still with me?), a state trooper came to the man's assistance. Thinking the trooper had come to arrest him, the thief began to kick and hit the cop and eventually fled to a nearby junkyard. Meanwhile, back at the convenience store, investigators were interviewing the two women who had been chased by the man when he walked in with the apparent intention of finishing the job. He was arrested immediately and charged with armed robbery, assault and battery, and assaulting a police officer while resisting arrest. Whew!

Ashes to Ashes

A woman in Memphis, Tennessee, learned that her husband was leaving her for another woman. Infuriated, she burned $186,000 in cash she found in his safety deposit box. A few weeks later, she was informed the box was being leased in her husband's name by another party. The woman's insurance company claimed no liability for the mix-up.

Jailhouse Rock

Two armed robbery suspects gained national notoriety as they had their photograph broadcast on the television show "America's Most Wanted." The photograph was taken of them in front of Elvis Presley's mansion, Graceland, in Memphis, Tennessee. Police discovered the photo, which had been left behind at the scene of a robbery in Clarksville, Arkansas.

Landscaper's Caper

— · — · —

Two yardbirds are now jailbirds after they were caught stealing sod in suburban Uniondale, New York. The thieves arrived at a vacant home at 2:00 a.m. and began rolling away the newly replaced grass. An insomniac neighbor saw them running off with a shopping cart full of the grass and called the police. As the thieves came back for another load, the cops were waiting with charges of petty larceny. One of the men claimed to be a landscaper.

Nesting Place

— · — · —

Police stopped a Baltimore man after watching him walk oddly down the street with bulging pants. Once stopped, the man revealed 21 live homing pigeons stuffed in his clothes.

You Dirty Rat

— · — · —

An 18-year-old man walked into a store in Scotland and held a rat up to the cashier's face. The man then instructed the cashier to "give me all your money or I'll sic my rat on you."

Minor Mix-up

A Schaumburg, Illinois, teen was questioned by a convenience store clerk as the minor tried to purchase a 12-pack of beer in the store. Seeing the young man's driver's license, the clerk exclaimed, "This isn't you!" The minor argued that it *was* his own face in the license photo. While the hair coloring was similar to that of the boy's, it was obvious to the clerk that his was a false I.D., for the boy had given him the clerk's own previously stolen driver's license.

The minor was speechless upon learning he had been caught red-handed, and fled to a car where three other youths were waiting. In his haste, however, he left his wallet behind, wherein his own driver's license was kept. The clerk notified police and the boy was apprehended a short time later.

Robber Suspected to Be Expecting

A Prestonsburg, Kentucky, woman faked pregnancy to lure the help of a man she then attempted to rob. The woman stuffed clothing into her blouse and stood beside the flat tire of her car until the good Samaritan pulled up to her and offered his assistance. A sheriff's lieutenant reported that the woman drew a gun and demanded he drive to a bank and withdraw money. As they pulled up to the bank, the driver "bailed and ran." The woman was found in a parking lot near the bank waiting to be picked up by her mother.

Joint Venture

— · — · —

All that talk about drug abuse was too much for one father as he attended a D.A.R.E. program at his son's suburban Ohio elementary school. The man snuck out to his car during the program for an illegal smoke. As with most D.A.R.E. activities, there was no shortage of police in attendance and the man was caught in the act in the school parking lot. He was arrested for possession of marijuana.

For a Good Time . . .

— · — · —

A 22-year-old Boothwyn, Pennsylvania, man was charged with burglary after police were called to the offices of a housing development by a 911 operator. The burglar had broken into the offices late that evening and attempted to call a 900 number for a phone sex service.

The man misdialed, inadvertently calling 911. Upon taking the call, the 911 operator became suspicious, and the call was automatically traced to the burglar.

Apologies for Pot in the Pocket

A Fayette County, Kentucky, grand jury member was arrested on charges of possession of marijuana and drug paraphernalia as he was frisked during a routine search at the courthouse. The man handed his jacket to the deputy sheriff as he entered the courtroom. When a hard object was felt in a pocket, further probing revealed the object to be a pipe, along with a bag of pot. The man was reported to be "apologetic" as he was handcuffed and led out of the courthouse and into the jailhouse. The trial was delayed briefly while a replacement juror was found.

Snort Cut to Stupidity

A Boynton Beach, Florida, man called police and reported that someone had broken into his home and stolen a tackle box wherein the ashes of his cremated sister were stored. Police determined that because nothing else was stolen, the thief possibly believed the ashes to be cocaine.

Sex, Lies and . . .
Broken Egg Shells?

After telling her husband and police that she had been raped at gunpoint, a Pontiac, Michigan, woman had a composite sketch made of the alleged rapist. The accused man saw his likeness on the television news and called the police. He claimed that they had had sex at his home, but it was not at all forced upon the woman. In fact, he said that she had even cooked him breakfast the following morning. When asked for proof, he produced several egg shells from his garbage which were covered with the woman's fingerprints. The police charged the woman with falsely reporting a rape.

One Thief with Two Stones

A man attempted to rob a Chandler, Arizona, convenience store with a T-shirt wrapped around his head, wielding large rocks. He then used the rocks as weapons to rob the store. Police pursued the suspect and later found him hiding in a tree. The rocks were recovered nearby.

Uh . . . Interpreter, Please!

A man walked into a Seattle check-cashing center wearing a wig and glued-on mustache and sideburns and handed the cashier a supposed hold-up note. The clerk later told police that it was a bunch of gibberish and he "couldn't even read it." The would-be thief became so frustrated and angry when his note could not be deciphered that he turned around and walked out.

One Hot Wedding!

A Topmost, Kentucky, woman was caught stuffing a $499 wedding dress under her coat the day of her wedding. The 18-year-old bride-to-be and two members of her wedding party were charged with shoplifting after police found more than $1500 worth of wedding merchandise in their car. Among the goods were suits, shirts, and ties for the groom and groomsmen, and apparel for the flower girl. They even thought to steal two velvet pillows for the ring bearers. The father of the bride posted bail and escorted his daughter out of jail. He then escorted her down the aisle of a neighborhood church, where the wedding went on as planned. There is no record of what they eventually wore at the wedding.

Trespasser with Taste

— · — · —

A stranger entered the home of a Cambridge, Ohio, woman and began cooking a pot roast in her kitchen. Despite the woman's protest, he helped himself to her utensils and started preparations for the roast. The man then left to get potatoes at the local grocery store. While he was gone, the woman called the police. They were there when the cook returned. After police questioned him, he admitted he did not know the woman, but only wanted her to have something to eat. He was told to leave, but insisted he stay to finish peeling the potatoes. The woman then insisted he leave, and the man was ushered out by police. The food was left at the woman's house.

Reward Share-amony

To collect a local Crime Stopper's cash reward, a Houston man turned over his colleague's name to police in connection with the recent murder of a convenience store clerk. It didn't dawn on the man that his "friend" would, in turn, turn him in as the alleged driver of the getaway car. In addition, the man's partner told police of a murder two months earlier which the would-be reward collector, the first fellow, allegedly committed. No reward money was collected for either man.

Cash Give-Away

Three North Fork, West Virginia, men were arrested in connection with a bank robbery. Days after the robbery, one of the men—formerly penniless—arrived at the local car dealership and paid cash for a brand-new Cadillac. This aroused suspicions in the car dealer, and the police were called to investigate.

Flop Cop

— · — · —

A police impersonator pulled over the Real McCoy and found himself in real trouble in St. Petersburg, Florida. The man, sporting a false badge and handcuffs, pulled over a detective using a flashing green light from the dashboard of his Cadillac. "I realized he wasn't a police officer," said the detective. "I told him I was a real police officer and he ought to get over to the curb. He was shocked." The man was arrested for impersonating an officer as well as driving while intoxicated.

Snatcher in the Rye

— · — · —

If anyone is guilty of stupidity in this story, it isn't the criminal. Still, it was too good not to include in this book. A television reporter from Owensboro, Kentucky, was doing a report from the local mall when someone ran by and snatched her purse. She had tossed it just out of camera range before doing her report. The purse was recovered later minus $50 in cash. Her report was on how to prevent one's purse from getting snatched during the busy Christmas shopping season.

Doughnut Holes in His Story

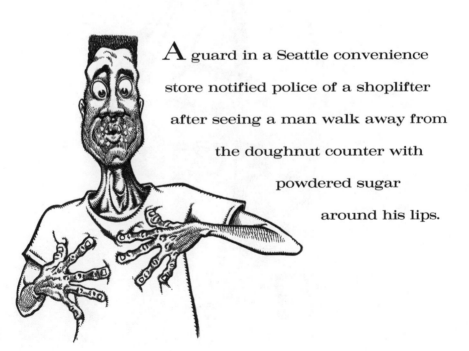

A guard in a Seattle convenience store notified police of a shoplifter after seeing a man walk away from the doughnut counter with powdered sugar around his lips.

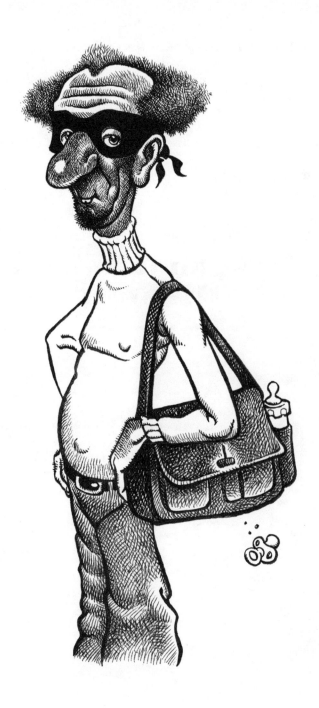

The Case of the Cry Baby and the Cat Burglar

One burglar in West Valley City, Utah, scores high in sensitivity but low in intellect. While allegedly burglarizing an apartment building, the man heard the incessant cries of a baby in an apartment down the hall from the one he was looting. He left the first apartment, broke into the second one where he heard the crying, and awakened the mother. He then instructed her to feed her baby and added that the little tyke's diaper may be soiled. The startled mother offered no response to his instructions. Irritated, the man left the room and changed the baby's diaper himself! He returned to the woman's bedroom where he lectured her on child care, then left. He was caught by police a short time later.

U-Turn into Destiny

Once pulled over by police, the driver of a car in Los Angeles immediately confessed to a recent drug-related murder. The 29-year-old man had led police on a 100 MPH chase down San Diego Freeway. Police began the pursuit after they merely saw the man make an illegal U-turn.

Tow Jam

— · — · —

The largest drug-related cash seizure to date in Kentucky occurred when $400,000 was found in a secret compartment underneath a car. The vehicle had broken down on a Laurel County highway. Police arrived and became a little suspicious when the driver arranged to have the car towed 930 miles to Miami. The tow would have cost $1,200 and the 10-year-old Mazda wasn't worth a penny over $500.

Caught by Compassion

— · — · —

A Las Vegas man robbed a couple at gunpoint and discovered that they only had twenty dollars between them. To prove he wasn't such a bad guy after all, he then went to a nearby convenience store and bought the couple a beer with his own money! Police were called and the man was eventually arrested.

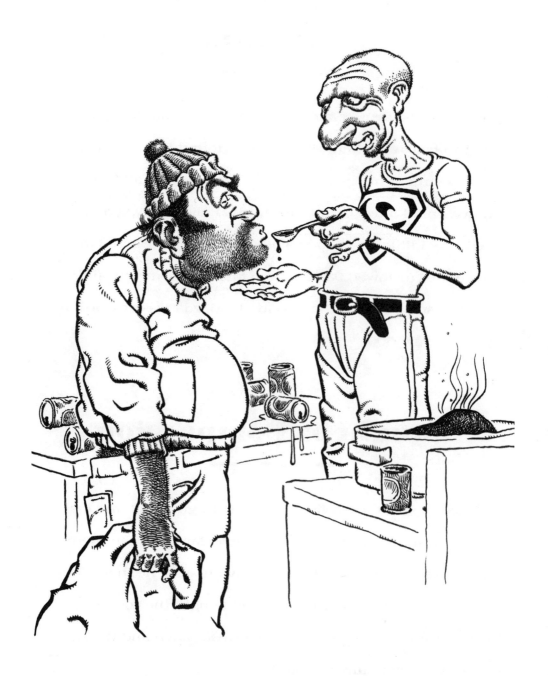

Breaking and Entering and Cooking

A woman in Wallingford, Connecticut, came home to find two strange men cooking a rib roast in her kitchen. She asked them who they were and why they were in her house. One of the men replied, "Hi. We're burglars." The woman added that the men "were drunk, really drunk."

Inside Joke

Somewhere in Kansas City, Missouri, there are some puzzled thieves. Two music stores in Kansas City reported the theft of hundreds of empty CD cases. The robbers, apparently thinking that CD's were inside, hastily made off with nearly 1,000 of the next-to-worthless plastic containers. More stores have begun taking the CD's out until purchased and storing them away for safekeeping.

Flipped Cop

One might think that a criminal would wish to control himself in the presence of police. This was not the case in Morehead, Kentucky, as a forestry officer drove past a car in which a passenger "gestured with his middle finger to the officer." The car was stopped and the angered officer questioned the young people. Suspecting substance abuse, he had their car searched. The driver of the car was subsequently arrested on alcohol and marijuana charges. One might say he was "fingered" by his not-so-bright passenger.

Rip-Off Tip-Off

A 24-year-old man was pulled over outside of Buffalo, New York, for driving at night without headlights. When the patrol man asked to see his license, the driver began nervously searching in the car and eventually produced a handful of cards and papers. Among the various identification, the patrolman found a note which contained the message, "I have a gun. Put all the money in the envelope quickly!" The note was linked to a heist two days earlier in which the man and a 25-year-old accomplice had robbed a Buffalo bank.

Frozen Fowl Play Uncovered in Booby Trap Snap

A middle-aged woman from Lausanne, Switzerland, has done her part to keep us abreast of the dangers of shoplifting. She attracted a crowd when she fell unconscious in a busy supermarket. An emergency medical team was then called to the store. Noticing the woman's brassiere to be extremely tight, a nurse on the team unhooked it to allow better respiration. As shoppers looked on, the root of the problem became manifest as a small, frozen chicken was extracted from the woman's bra. She regained consciousness moments later. The medical team determined that she had passed out due to the cold.

Tell-Tale Pants

A Hicksville, New York, man was arrested for shoplifting at a downtown pet store after a clerk heard chirping sounds coming from the man's pants. When confronted about the noise, he reluctantly produced two healthy, but frightened lovebirds from his pocket.

What's Love Got to Do with It?

— ˙ — ˙ —

A 58-year-old woman in Swansy, Wales, was robbed by a masked, gun-wielding man who had broken into her house. During the confrontation the man's mask slipped. The woman was shocked to discover that it was her own son! She told the press later, "I still love him, in a way." Her love didn't stop her from pressing charges, however, and the man is now doing 15 months in jail for aggravated assault.

Too Many Thieves, Not Enough Victims

— ˙ — ˙ —

An 88-year-old woman was robbed of $200 in cash from her car while stopping to ask for directions in Boca Raton, Florida. A passerby reached into the car and grabbed the money while the woman was stopped at the curb. The female thief, 31, turned to run with the loot when two teenagers grabbed the money from her hands. Witnesses at the scene were prompted to call 911 after the 31-year-old woman began screaming. The police arrived and arrested all three thieves and returned the money to the elderly woman from whom it was first taken.

This, Too, Shall Pass

A Los Angeles clerk witnessed a woman shoplifting a piece of jewelry. The clerk promptly called the store manager. They were about to confront the woman when she took the jewelry from her purse and swallowed it. The manager, then showing true intestinal fortitude, escorted the shoplifter to a bathroom in the back of the store. Once there, he demanded she enter and not come out until she had the jewelry in hand. Apparently, everything came out okay, but there is no record of how long the manager had to wait.

Squad-Car Serenade

Police in Oceanside, California, were not charmed or amused as they listened to a risqué rap song—coming from their own radios! Officers traced the song to a fenced-in lot just behind the police station where the rapper was singing into the radio of an unattended squad car. The song was filled with "things he likes to do, most of them obscene and punctuated with profanity," according to the police report. A police spokesman said he was under the influence of narcotics during his radio debut.

You Can't Steal Just One

Two men attacked and robbed the driver of a Vegas Chips truck in Las Vegas, Nevada, after they discovered the truck did not contain poker chips, but *potato* chips. The driver was told to get out of the truck, open the door, and "turn over the chips." Puzzled, the driver opened the door and stood back to let the men take what they wanted. When they saw the supply of snacks, the would-be poker players snapped. They hit the driver over the head, stole his keys, and took an undisclosed amount of money.

The driver was not seriously injured. A company spokesperson claims the trucks are clearly identified as potato chip carriers. The logo on the sides of the truck shows an open bag with potato chips as well as poker chips spilling out. Vegas Chips claims to have never had a previous problem with mistaken identity.

Every Dog Has Its Day

After tripping an alarm, a 14-year-old burglar in Phoenix, Arizona, found himself surrounded by police. The boy barricaded himself in the home and refused to surrender. After some time, police threatened to send in the K-9 Corps. The boy still refused to come out until he heard vicious barking just outside the door. "Don't let the dog come in!" he screamed. "I'm coming out!" As the young thief surrendered, he was shown the source of the barking: one of the police officers who had been crouched by the door.

Habitual Offenders

Four former nuns who had left the order because of hard work and low pay were arrested in Ecuador for possession of narcotics. The Columbian women each had large packets of cocaine strapped to their legs beneath their Roman Catholic-issued habits. They were stopped by police and questioned in Quinto's International Airport after officers saw the nuns "walking like ducks." They were charged with drug trafficking and sent to jail.

Down in the Mouth

A Camden, New Jersey, thief put someone else's money where his mouth was as he was pursued by police in a local check-cashing center. The victim of the crime had just cashed two checks totaling $500 when a thief grabbed the money and ran toward the door. The victim yelled to an employee who quickly activated the locks on the electronic doors, locking the thief inside. As a struggle ensued between the victim and the robber, police were called to the scene. The criminal, seeing the approaching police, began to eat the $100 bills. Witnesses reported the man stuffed three of the bills in his mouth "and began chewing fast." He swallowed two of the bills, but a third was yanked from his mouth. The other $200 was found on his person. He was arrested for robbery and aggravated assault.

Getaway Glitches

Planes,
Trains
and
Clod mobiles

They Never Forget a . . . Face

An Albuquerque, New Mexico, man was literally caught with his pants down as he fled a jewelry store with stolen merchandise. As he turned and ran, his pants dropped to his ankles, causing him to stumble and trip. The robber then dropped his gun and most of the stolen jewelry. He finally managed to gather his "things" together and escape in a stolen truck. He was spotted an hour later and identified by witnesses who had seen his *barely* successful escape from behind. His identity was further reinforced as his pants once again dropped to the ground as he was being led away in handcuffs.

99 Bottles of Beer in the Street . . .

In an apparent attempt to "lift" his spirits, a Huntington, Indiana, man was seen driving down the street hauling 30 cases of beer—on a forklift! Police followed a trail of spilled beer cases to the forklift, not far from where it and the beer were stolen. After questioning the man, police discovered the beer to be taken from the City Beverage Company in Huntington. The man had driven six blocks and was almost home when police pulled him over. He was arrested on a preliminary charge of possession of stolen property.

On the Brink of Stupidity

— · — · —

Two New York City men, in the attempted robbery of a Brinks armored truck, held the guards at gunpoint, confiscated their weapons, forced them into the back of the truck, and drove away. Using his cellular phone (which the robbers apparently had not seen), one of the guards promptly called police and informed them of the vehicle's every turn. Police were soon on the trail of the truck and the thieves were apprehended.

Thief in TRAINing

— · — · —

After robbing a rural Wisconsin grocery store, the loot-carrying thief headed back to his car, which was parked a short distance away across some railroad tracks. He approached the crossing but was dismayed to see an oncoming train. While the man stood waiting for the train, store clerks called police. Finally the last car of the train rolled by, but the thief was surprised to see police waiting . . . on the other side of the tracks!

Naked Aggression

An elderly woman looked out her window to see two skin-head young men attempting to steal her car. Throwing all caution to the wind, she darted out of her house and onto the front lawn, yelling and waving her fists in the air. The young men gave the woman a startled look and then scampered away. She stood proudly in her yard

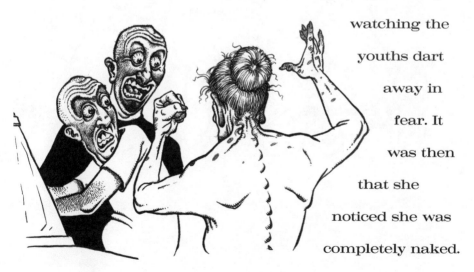

watching the youths dart away in fear. It was then that she noticed she was completely naked.

Bad Defense

A 23-year-old Lexington, North Carolina, man was seen running from the store where he had allegedly just pilfered an entire bag of cigarettes. With the loot in tow, he ran past a nearby field where the Lexington Senior High School football team was practicing. The tobacco thief was chased down and tackled by no less than thirty of the team's players, who held him down until police arrived.

Hangin' Five to Ten

A family in St. Paul, Minnesota, was blocked in their car and approached by two men who demanded money. When they saw the rolled-up windows and locked doors, the robbers became violent, jumping on top of the car and pounding on the roof. The family sped off with the two men clinging to the roof of the vehicle. One of the robbers was still there when they screeched to a stop in front of police headquarters. He was arrested immediately.

Down in the Dumps

An escaped convict attempted to hide from police by entering the back of a garbage truck. The convict soon discovered his hideaway to be a garbage compression compartment which the driver of the truck activated while the prisoner was inside! He was found in a pile of garbage at a landfill by a local farmer. Other than a few broken bones and a bruised ego, the prisoner was okay. He was returned to jail to finish his sentence.

Wheels of Misfortune

Two Chicago boys might have planned their escape route a little better as they ran from the store they had just robbed using fake guns. A local police precinct was having its bicycle patrol tryouts nearby, and upon seeing the fleeing youths, a few cops pedaled away and ran the boys down.

Car Jackass

Four young men picked the wrong vehicle to steal one busy Christmas shopping day. The youths were stalking through a mall parking lot in Lakeland, Florida, when one of the boys jumped into a white van and began to turn the key to start it. He was surprised to see three policemen in the back of the van with surveillance equipment. The officers were there to watch for car thieves. They didn't expect their set-up to work so well, however.

"It was hard to keep from laughing," one officer was reported to say.

One Good Turn . . .

A Portland, Oregon, woman was driving home one day when she recognized the car in front of her to be her previously stolen sedan. She stayed with the car for about 20 minutes, following it to a residential neighborhood. Two men got out and entered a house a few doors down. The woman ran to her long-lost car and drove to a phone where she called police. It turns out that the car thieves were also burglars, and they had entered the house to rob it. When they came out, they found their getaway car "restolen," and the police were on their way.

Next Time, Steal a Car First!

A Hartford, Connecticut, man, needing assistance to outrun police, called a local taxi company to take him and the loot of a recent robbery somewhere quickly. Suspecting the police were trailing him, he frantically called the company four times, urging them to hurry. The cab driver never arrived to see the man handcuffed and escorted to the police car. The robbery suspect was heard to say, "I'm never going to use that company again," as he was taken to jail.

His Getaway Got Away

— · — · —

The robber of a bank in New Haven, Connecticut, was a bit surprised as he exited the bank with his booty—only to discover that his getaway vehicle had been stolen during the hold-up. He had left it idling outside while he went in to make the "withdrawal." The villain-turned-victim was caught by police as he attempted to escape on foot.

The Good, the Bad, and the Hungry

— · — · —

An escaped prisoner fled to the home of an elderly couple in Braden, Tennessee, brandishing a shotgun. The 73-year-old woman saw the convict from the window of her neighbor's home as he pointed the gun at her husband. Unshaken, the woman told the neighbor to call the police, then went outside. She greeted the man, insisting he come inside for breakfast. He acknowledged he hadn't eaten in three days. While she cooked scrambled eggs and bacon, the woman preached to him about Jesus and prayed for him as they sat down to eat. While the man ate, the woman's husband disabled his truck so he couldn't escape. "Put your gun down," said the woman. "I'm a Christian and I don't want no violence." The convict followed her instructions "like a little child" and eventually surrendered to police. He was taken back to prison, where he was serving a 25-year term for murder.

It Was So Nice of Him to Drop By!

Having just robbed a sandwich shop, a St. Paul, Minnesota, man was surprised to see his escape route interrupted by a swarm of police officers. His poorly planned post-hold-up run led him past a police precinct during a shift change.

Bank Blunders

**Thieves who were
caught through no vault
of their own.**

No Deposit, No Return

A Seattle man was arrested at a neighborhood bank when he attempted to open a savings account and deposit a large sum of cash in the bank. Police were alerted by one of the tellers at the bank who recognized the man as the same one who had robbed the bank only 48 hours earlier.

Robbing Banks Can Be a Real Drag

Hoping he would trick the police into looking for a female bank robber, a man showed up in a Spartanburg, South Carolina, bank dressed as a woman. Wearing a wig, makeup, high heels, and a "shocking pink dress," the robber entered the bank and demanded money. He might have been a bit more convincing, however, if he had shaved the beginnings of a beard from his face.

Cause for Alarm

Police in northern Japan were called to a midnight bank robbery in progress after the bank's alarm had been triggered by the burglar. The startled robber was found inside and was later identified as the bank manager! As he was being handcuffed, he explained to police that he forgot the bank had an alarm.

Amazing Disgrace

A comedy of errors took place in a Kirkersville, Ohio, bank when an armed 77-year-old, 5'2" retiree came and robbed the place of $26,000. The bank's video photos showed the man struggling to climb over the bank counter, moving a stool to assist him, getting his feet tangled up in the stool, and eventually raising his nylon stocking mask so he could see to gather the loot. The latter act exposed the identity of the man, and he was later arrested as a suspect in connection with the armed robbery.

Forging Ahead

Two Redwood City, California, teens were charged with forgery and possession of stolen property when they were caught at a bank attempting to cash a stolen check. The youths, ages 16 and 17, had allegedly broken into a car across from their high school and swiped the owner's checkbook. They forged the owner's name and wrote the check out for $250 and went to cash it at the Wells Fargo bank. The teenagers were turned over to police after the cashier recognized the check to be from her own father's checkbook.

Deposit Slip-Up

— . — . —

After handing the cashier a hold-up note, the robber of a suburban Cincinnati bank took the money and ran, leaving the note behind. Turning the piece of paper over, the cashier noticed it was a deposit slip from someone's personal checkbook. After a little investigation, police discovered the slip to belong to none other than the robber himself! They simply took note of the thief's account number and address and followed him home.

Strategy Stops Star-Struck Stickup

— . — . —

The 22-year-old robber of a bank in Quincy, Illinois, surrendered after a six-hour standoff with police. The bank's executive vice-president, who was being held hostage by the thief, faked a heart attack and convinced the robber to surrender. The hostage explained that if he died of a heart attack, the bank robbery would be too gruesome for Hollywood, should they want to buy the movie rights to his story. He told the robber that if he got medical treatment and survived, he could help him sell the story and make both of them rich and famous.

Bomb Attempt Bombs

A Madison, Wisconsin, sheriff's bomb squad was called to a bank after the alarm was set off by a fleeing would-be robber. The squad found a bottle of nitroglycerin connected to a detonator next to a safe. The criminal left prematurely after discovering the extension cord for the detonator was three feet short of the nearest electrical outlet.

Seen at the Scene

Caught by Carelessness

Crime Can Be Taxing

The man who robbed a mobile home in Canal Fulton, Ohio, was surprised to see police at his home only moments after the crime. He was even more surprised to see his W-2 tax forms in the hands of the police when they arrived. The clueless criminal had dropped them at the mobile home during the robbery. The forms were filled out, complete with his name, address and social security number.

There is no record of whether or not the thief reported robbery proceeds as income.

A Flash in the Can

Police in Charles City, Virginia, ran through the darkness after a man who had robbed a convenience store. They caught up with him about a mile away from the crime. The capture was facilitated by the criminal's new shoes: LA Gear's "Lite Gear" athletic shoes, which flash with light as the shoe makes contact with the ground. Police report that they "just followed the shoes."

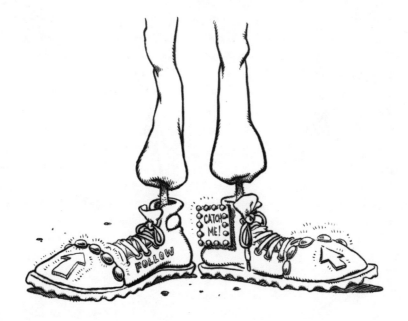

Probed Putty Points Police to Perpetrator

Police in Toronto, Canada, are using the aid of Silly Putty in their pursuit of a burglar. After breaking into the office space of a communications company, the thief took time out of the robbery to fondle a wad of Silly Putty located there. An employee noticed the fresh fingerprints in the putty and turned it over to police for evidence.

Don't Leave a Crime Scene without It

After an 18-year-old Hawthorne, California, man called police to report that his wallet had been stolen, he was promptly arrested for armed robbery. Why? Well, the young man had absentmindedly dropped the wallet while fleeing the convenience store he had robbed a few days earlier. Police were holding the wallet as evidence when the thief called to report it missing.

Video Tracking

South Haven, Indiana, police were called to investigate the break-in of a video store late one evening. After talking with the owners of the store, the policemen noticed a trail of candy wrappers, video game cases, and empty soda cans just outside the back door of the building. Following the trail, police were led to a campsite in the woods nearby, where they found pillows, sleeping bags, and more goods stolen from the store. Also found at the site was a wallet containing the identification of one of the three boys later arrested for the burglary. They were 10, 12, and 14 years of age.

Framed by His Own Frames

While police were investigating the robbery of a bank outside Chicago, one of the bank employees produced a pair of glasses the robber had absentmindedly left behind. An identification number inscribed on the frame showed that the glasses were a prison-issue prescription. After calling the nearby prison, police tracked down the soon-to-be reconvicted ex-con within one hour.

Trails, You Lose

— · — · —

Two teenage boys from Toledo, Ohio, were arrested for the armed robbery of a gas station near their home. Police had only to follow the trail of money the boys had dropped, starting behind the station and leading to a nearby trailer park, where they found the two boys, their guns, and what was left of the money.

The Next Best Thing to Being There

— · — · —

A Vancouver, Canada, man robbed a warehouse of thousands of dollars worth of skate and ski boards. While checking out the scene of the crime, police found the thief's home phone pager on the floor. They needed only to dial the number displayed in the pager to find him.

A Remote Possibility of Getting Caught

This criminal was not only stupid but lazy, too. A 24-year-old man was arrested in Grapevine, Texas, for stealing a television from a local residence. He may have gotten away with the crime had he not returned for the remote control. Police were there when he arrived the second time.

Snow Shoe Stupidity

Old Man Winter assisted officers in Long Island, New York, as they searched for the robber of a nearby store. Long Island detectives simply followed the thief's footprints they found in a blanket of freshly fallen snow that led from the door of the establishment. They caught up with the criminal as he was still walking a few blocks away.

Paper or Plastic?

A Jacksonville, Florida, convenience store was almost robbed by a man with a paper bag over his head. Two holes had been cut out for visibility, but the bag twisted a bit during the attempted robbery. When the man tried to put it back in place, the bag ripped open, revealing his identity. The clerk then recognized him as a regular customer. The clerk reported, "I yelled, 'Bob!' Then he ran away."

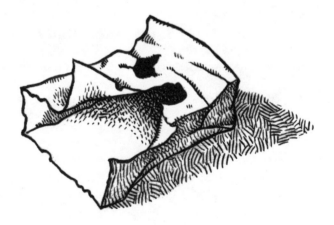

DISORGANIZED CRIME
Hall of Blame

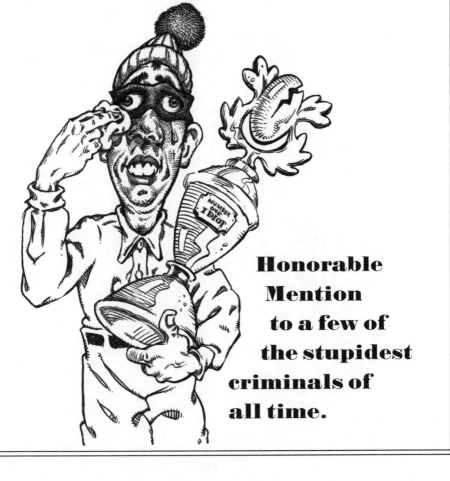

Honorable Mention to a few of the stupidest criminals of all time.

Weeded Out

Most of us know that drug cultivation is illegal. But a West Goshen, Pennsylvania, man must have suffered from a short-term memory loss when he called police to complain that eight of his marijuana plants had been stolen. The police then arrested the man on three drug counts.

In the Dark

— · — · —

A 21-year-old man from Texas City, Texas, was arrested after police caught him attempting to drag a newspaper vending machine to his running car. As the officers walked up to the man, he quickly stopped and pretended to be reading the front cover of the newspaper inside. "I was dragging it over here so I could read the paper better," he explained. When one of the policemen pointed out that the light was better where the machine was, the man exclaimed, "I read better in the dark." He was charged with misdemeanor theft.

It's Curtains for
These Curtain Thieves

— · — · —

One male and two female shoplifters entered a home supplies store, stuffed some curtains into bags, and attempted to escape through three separate exits. If the thieves had read the sign outside, which welcomed attendees to the Store Detective Convention, they might have thought twice. All three of the criminals were immediately caught by several attending officers.

Muddy Reasoning

Two men were charged with the theft of a large electronic dart game from a bar outside Cudahy, Wisconsin. The machine was so heavy that when they put it into their pick-up truck, it sunk into the mud in the parking lot outside the tavern. With the stolen  machine still in the truck, and their tires submerged in mud, one of the men called a local sheriff to get a tow. A policeman later told reporters, "They didn't put a real lot of thought into this."

Mugger Gets Real Sense of "Dootie"

A Los Angeles woman was walking her poodle one evening when a mugger attacked her from behind, knocked her to the ground, and grabbed the plastic bag she was carrying. She suffered a broken arm in the scuffle, but remained good-natured about the incident, noting the mugger made off with nothing more than a bag of poodle poop. "You have to be considerate of your neighbors," she said in reference to cleaning up after her pet. "I only regret that I did not have more to give him."

Duplex Dunce

— · — · —

A 20-year-old Norfolk, Virginia, man was arrested and charged with the burglary and arson of his neighbor's house. He allegedly broke into his neighbor's house, stole a TV, VCR, and camera, then set the house on fire to obliterate any evidence of the crime. His neighbor's house, however, was half of the duplex where he lived, and when his place also suffered damage from the fire, firefighters entered to find his neighbor's stuff inside.

Drive-thru Debauchery

— · — · —

A 24-year-old man was arrested after robbing a Hardee's restaurant in Caderburg, Wisconsin. It seemed that nothing went right for the thief that day. To start off, he parked his car in the drive-thru and left it in the wrong direction. He then went to the men's room at a gas station next door. By this time there were frustrated drivers who wished to go in the drive-thru but couldn't, and they went inside Hardee's to complain. The man then entered the restaurant and robbed it of $650. Upon returning to his car, he discovered he had left his keys in the gas station men's room. The police were waiting for him when he came back to his car with the keys.

In Between Jobs

A Dorchester, Massachusetts, man identified as the armed robber who shot and wounded a store manager claims he is the victim of mistaken identity. He was positively identified, however, by two witnesses of the robbery in a photo lineup. The man was caught when he returned to the scene of the crime to apply for a job and was recognized by a store employee.

Silence Is Golden

A New York street vendor prompted the natural curiosity of police as they heard him exclaiming, "Stolen Gold! Stolen Gold!" in a very loud voice. They approached the man and after some discussion, took him and his inventory to the police station for further examination.

Crackpot Businessman

P olice were alerted to a man in Richmond, Virginia, who was passing out business cards on the street which read:

> Head Crack! Head Crack! Weight Is So Good
> True Pipers Will Be Back! Cook EM Up/Powder;
> 9 p.m.–12 a.m. Mon.–Sun. Walking corner to corner with boom box.

The man was arrested for possession of cocaine.

Something up His Sleeve

A 16-year-old boy from Fort Wayne, Indiana, was taken to juvenile court and accused of stealing the jacket of another boy. The expensive athletic jacket was adorned with the color and logo of Penn State University. The 16-

year-old claimed that he indeed had a jacket just like the one the other boy had described, but that it wasn't stolen. In fact, he had even worn it to court that day. When asked for proof that the jacket was his, the young plaintiff took the jacket, turned one sleeve inside out, and showed the judge his own name printed on the fabric.

A Confession of Stupidity

Suspected of snatching a purse from a 76-year-old woman, a Minneapolis man was brought in to police headquarters. Police routinely lined up several suspects for identification by the victim. When the man was asked to turn his baseball hat around with the bill toward the front, he declined, saying he would keep it on backwards, as "that's the way I had it on when I took the purse." The lineup was discontinued.

An Appetite for Crime

A Columbus, Ohio, man was arrested for robbing pizza deliverers outside his home. He would call the pizza shop, give them his order, and then wait outside. When they came with his pizza, he would take it and all their money! The pizza thief wasn't too hard for police to find because each time he had called the shop, he had given his real name, address, and phone number.

Crash Course in Common Sense

— · — · —

Two Rockville, Maryland, college students—a male and a female—were expelled from school for buying and selling academic work. The female paid the male student $200 to take an exam in her stead. They were caught after word got back to the dean's office that the young woman was suing her partner in crime to get her money back, because he had flunked the exam!

Double-take Debunks Dual Identity

— · — · —

A man walked into a pawnbroker's office and tried to cash a $789 income tax refund check. The man presented the check, made payable to an Ernestine and Robert Hays, along with an ID card giving his name as Ernestine and Robert Hays. After being questioned by the puzzled pawnbroker, the man explained that his mother had been expecting twins, and when he was the only baby that came out, she went ahead and gave him both names! The pawnbroker tried to hold his laughter, excused himself, and called the police. The man was arrested and the check was returned to the real Ernestine and Robert Hays.

In Over His Head

A 19-year-old man was arrested in Gadsden, Alabama, when his robbery attempt was interrupted by police. The young would-be robber was caught in a convenience store wearing a pair of panty hose over his head, a pair of socks over his hands, and a large butcher knife in his pocket. Police entered the store to make a purchase and became suspicious when they saw the young man in the back of the store, having just put on the panty hose.

Upon seeing the cops, the thief pulled an item from a shelf and pretended to be shopping. And it may have been convincing if he hadn't been wearing those panty hose over his head.

Dream Scheme
Loses Steam

— · — · —

Using a false identity, a man sent letters to 100,000 restaurants all over the country claiming that while eating in their establishment, a waiter had carelessly spilled a drink on his clothes, which had subsequently cost him $9.00 to have cleaned. The man calculated that if all the restaurants responded, the scheme would make him a millionaire. After being tipped off to police and questioned, the man confessed, admitting that after he spent $29,000 in postage, only 20 restaurants responded, giving him a total of $180 in "earnings."

Make It Out to "Stupid"

— · — · —

An 18-year-old Baltimore man broke into a home, assaulted the owner, and began to search the home for money. After finding only $11.50 in cash, the thief asked,

"How do you pay your bills?" "By check," replied the frightened woman. The robber then demanded she write him a check for $50.00. "Whom shall I make it out to?" asked the woman. The thief then gave his full name to the woman as she wrote it down in her checkbook. Having that information, the police later found the brainless thug and arrested him.

How Do I Kill Thee? Let Me Input the Ways

An officer of the U.S. Marine Corps was charged with his wife's murder after investigators entered his home computer system and found a file he had created and saved as "MURDER." Contained in the software was some pretty hard evidence that pointed to him as the culprit. Among the findings was a 26-step plan for the murder, with reminders and alibis, and the question, "How do I kill her?"

From Penn State to the State Pen?

A testy female student at Penn State University unwittingly turned herself in to local police when her plan to outsmart the university failed. The woman complained to police that she had given a fellow classmate a $1,200 stereo as payment for taking a final exam for her. He flunked the exam and she wanted her stereo back. The police turned the two students over to the university, reminding the woman that it is illegal to buy or sell academic work in the state of Pennsylvania.

No Room Service Where He's Going

A 28-year-old man was arrested for the robbery of a Best Western motel clerk in Cherokee, Iowa. He was easily tracked down, as he had registered as a guest only minutes before and given the motel his real name and address.

You Can't Trust Anyone These Days

A man jumped into a woman's car in Lakewood, California, and commanded her to go to the automatic teller machine, withdraw money, and give it to him. The woman asked him if she could simply go to a supermarket and cash a check. Not wanting to be difficult, the man agreed. The driver parked her car outside the store,

went inside, and promptly called the police. The man
was waiting in the car when police arrived.

What? No Drive-Thru?

Police were called to a bank when a woman told them
she was being robbed. The four robbers were waiting outside in a truck after they kidnapped her and threatened
to kill her unless she went into her bank, took out
money, and gave it to them. They were still waiting
patiently in the truck when police arrived.

You Said a Mouthful!

A Seattle man was caught one evening trying to steal gas from the tank of a mobile home, when the owner of the vehicle was awakened to the sound of someone spitting and choking just outside his window. He went outside to find a man curled up on the ground a few yards away. The gas thief had hastily placed his syphon hose in the wrong tank and withdrawn not gas, but the contents of the vehicle's sewage tank.

Ron Bell is a writer and illustrator who lives with his wife, Sharon, and their four children in Kentucky. He studied design and illustration at Brigham Young University and has taught illustration at the University of Kentucky. He worked for a brief time as an artist at Hallmark Cards until he was asked to draw "one too many snugly kittens," at which point he left to pursue his freelance career.

Rob N. Pilfer is *Disorganized Crime*'s poster boy for stupid criminals. He has asked that his real name not be used and that artist's renderings be shown in lieu of photographs. A three-time graduate of the Scared *Smart* program, he is now in a seven-step rehabilitation program and seems to be improving . . . somewhat.

Have you read any stories of stupid criminals? If so, please send them to the author c/o LONGSTREET PRESS for possible inclusion in the next volume of *Disorganized Crime*. Include your name, the clipped articles, and the name and date of the publication in which they appeared.